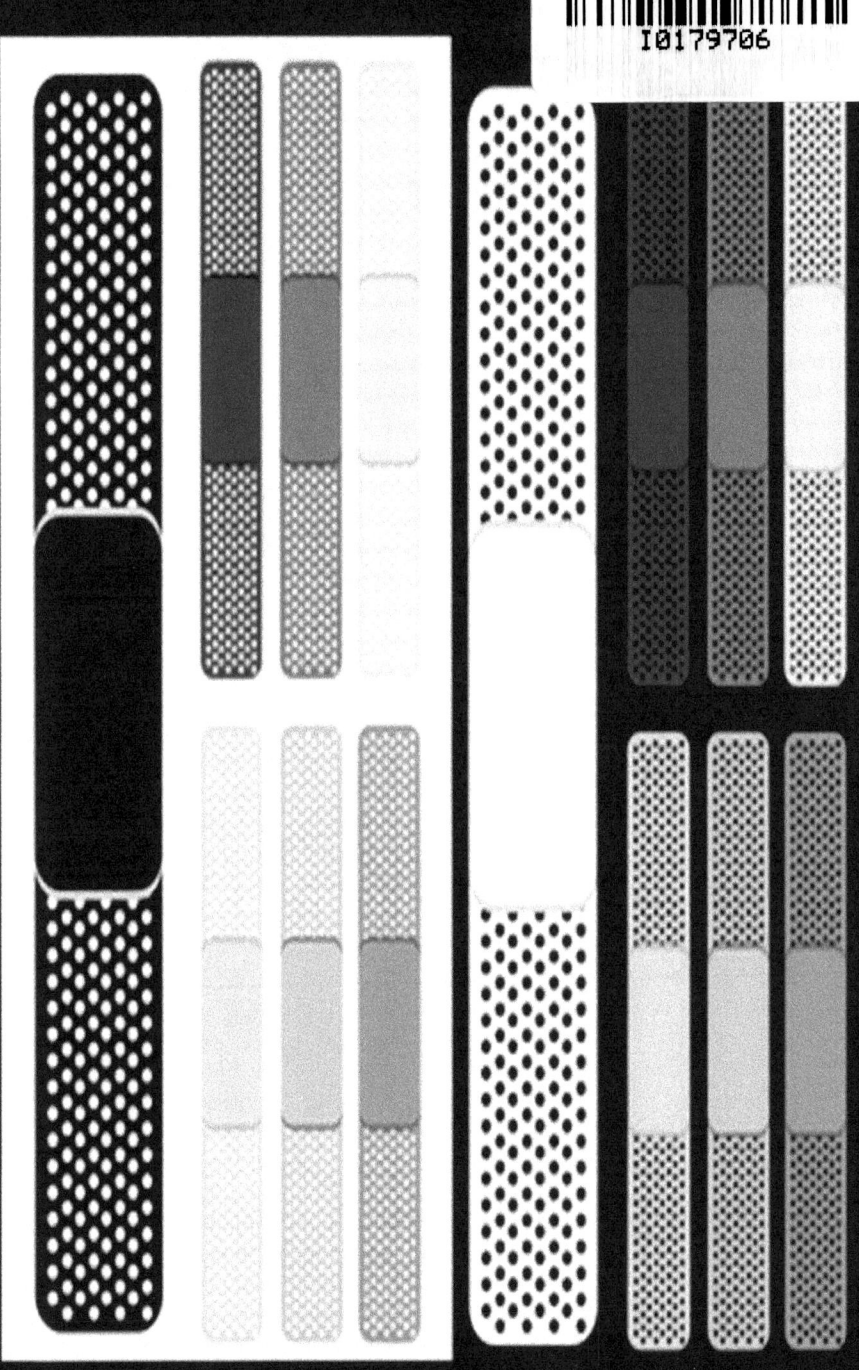

Unwrapped

The BareBack Anthology

BareBackPress

This is a work of fiction. The characters, incidents, and dialogue are the products of the authors' imaginations and are not to be construed as real. Any resemblance to actual events or person, living or dead, is entirely coincidental.

BareBackPress
Hamilton, Ontario, Canada
For enquires visit www.barebackpress.com
Contact BareBackPress at press@barebacklit.com

Cover layout by Choi Yunnam
Poems collected by Peter Jelen

This page cannot legibly accommodate all the copyright notices. All work appearing in this book is the property of the respective contributors. .No part of this book may be used or reproduced in any manner whatsoever without written permission, except in the case of brief quotations embodied in critical articles and reviews. For information address BareBackPress.

COPYRIGHT © 2013 BAREBACKPRESS
All RIGHTS RESERVED
ISBN-13: 978-0988075047
ISBN-10: 0988075040

CONTENTS

Nick Ransom
He Spoke of Death
6-6-12

David Whippman
Marriage Straight to Video
The Move

Ben Kandov
Interpersonal Relation
Freedom

Mike Algera
Taking it Up the Ass
Dear telemarketing agent

Rebecca Stone
An Excerpt from Ernie Lobe's Romantic Journal
Another Excerpt from Ernie Lobe's Romantic Journal

Marsha A. Temlock
Mammogram
The Seltzer Man

Yevgeniy Levitskiy
No Refunds
Soften

Steven Mayoff
This Is My Status
Motifs

Kevin Thornburgh
Young courtesan
Once

Larry Schug
Runaway Tractor
Lesson From a Zen Master

Sylvester Pilgrim
Timeless Resonance
Peerless Lucidity

Rebecca Halton
Guitar Man
Joggers

Mike Thorn
Cast Light
15th Ave Funeral

Jacob Nantz
Love, Life, and other Games Lost
Answers found on a Café Corner near Oriel College

Katherine Givens
Shades of Time
Hidden Beauty

Jason Barry
Buntings
Remembering Francisco

Donna Hawks
iWorld
One Night Stand

Sebastiaan Bonnarens
Horology
A Strange Witness

Brendan Sullivan
Chelsea Morning
river

Keith Kennedy
All Beauty
With boots on – naked in the woods besides

Roberta Swereda
highs
subs

Rebecca Rose Taylor
What I Can't Say
Relocating

Alyssa Cooper
When names held power
The Pen

Sandra Langer
Fireside
Killer

Melissa June
My Crazed Mind
My Minds Maze

Kellen Davis
happy town
never-never

Sam Silva
I Work for You with My Neurotic Mind
Computer Poetry till Morning

Ted Bussy
Tourists
Gift

Sonnet Mondal
Blue-Collar Twister
Reddened Sky

Maria Emmanuelle Arnidou
Dismantle
Your Light

Poppy Taylor
The Politics of Death
Cry Me A Daddy...

Darren Simon
Picfecturing Spontaneity
Language Arts

Nemoi Enpoj
Mirrors
My Dinner

Shannon Lyndsy
Impressions of an Ex-Pat
Eternal Death

Shannon Shuster
the way of the world.
trigger.

Howie Good
Tramp! Tramp! Tramp!
Pornocupia

Tony Mulas
A Time of Innocence
Mr. Baraxa

A Few Words:

BareBack Magazine began a little over a year ago in January 2012. Essentially, the goal was to find honest, unpretentious, sincere writing by people who simply love the craft. And this anthology is a demonstration of that.

**Enjoy,
P.J.
Editor**

Unwrapped

Unwrapped

Unwrapped

Unwrapped

Unwrapped

Unwrapped

Unwrapped

To those who aren't afraid to ride through life bareback.

He Spoke of Death
Nick Ranson

He spoke of murder like poetry,
Of hands on hearts,
Deep inside of forbidden secrets.

He whispered words like "torture",
"Collapse"
And "eviscerate"
As if they were the sweetest things imaginable.

A thousand horrors roiling in my mind,
An insufferable urge to destroy,
To hurt
To inflict

Coupled with an incomparable joy
Found only
In one other.

His words were red and lush,
Covering things previously unknown
At once shadowed and enlightened;
Simultaneously brilliant,
And terrible.
Absolutely beautiful.

He spoke of death like religion,
Like the last great adventure;
As some barely-conceived bit of brilliance.

He spoke of death as if he'd tasted it,
Somehow feeling my experiences through our bond,
Knowing more than me about things I've come so close to,
Dipped just deep enough into.

He spoke of beautiful,
Terrible things.

Of our mutual desires,
Shared nightmares
And combined promises.

6-6-12
Nick Ranson

Curl close to me,
With your eyes as full as your mind,
As strong as your arms
Spearing
Past the point of discomfort,
Into the realm of unreality,
I find myself falling into an ecstatic kind of complacency
When your skin comes against mine.
Dig deep into me,
And pull out all the best parts,
The reusable, the repurposed
The ones you seem to love the most.
Tearing
Away the years and memories,
Leaving something warmer and infinitely more
Receptive
Open in strange new ways only you could appreciate,
Only you could really see

And its fine that way.
These new alterations,
Improvements in the system,
These are all your work
Why shouldn't you reap all these strange little seeds you've sewn?
Pushed deep into the meat of things,
The grating hard-pan cracked to expose something living
In spite of everything.
Bend down to me,

Swaying like a twisting, lovely oak
Full arms and warmth around me
Meeting the edge of everything.
Keep
Holding me down,
Holding me back,
Holding me together.
Everything is necessary,
Each word and each second
Is all we have.
And in the end, that's everything.

About Nick Ransom:

Inspired by everything from long nights spent watching the city, to quiet afternoons in the cemetery, Nick Ransom is a hopeless romantic at heart. When not writing or making art, Ransom can usually be found guzzling massive quantities of tea, hoarding Magic the Gathering cards, or rambling about any number of things with his partner.

THE MOVE
David Whippman

The room and I did not choose each other:
circumstances have shipwrecked me here
in this shaped vacancy which seems
geometrically indifferent to my needs,
uncomfortable as new shoes. Reluctantly
I unpack, stick posters on walls, the banners
of an occupying army. Now I must wait
as if to be rescued. In time, the room
will contain friends, be warm on winter nights,
acceptably surround me as the radio sings
of possible relationships. By the time I leave
this space will be a perfect fit for me.

MARRIAGE STRAIGHT TO VIDEO
David Whippman

When it was obvious things weren't working out
(neither of us good on the other's cue)
of course we tried to talk. But I mean we just weren't
scriptwriters. Still... this nomination!
Yes, the role was cathartic.
I have to thank the director, for knowing
Exactly how much grief to cut.

About David Whippman:

Dave Whippman is British, in his early 60s, now retired having spent most of his working life in healthcare. He writes articles, poems and stories. His work has appeared in the small press, women's magazines, healthcare journals and newspapers. He currently lives in Blackpool Lancs.

Interpersonal Relation
Ben Kandov

Pleading will not change modern fate which is
Ordained as it occurs;
You may only watch it unfold, unsure.
The humble brown of your contemplation
Has been speedily reverting red – be wary if you'd prefer:
They can easily tell.
Your "Fates" have each two eyes,
A quarter and growing pairs of them kept behind glasses,
And a disproportionate number: extremely partial, moody,
insecure:
Mirrors of your own misjudgment
Times innumerable and most unknowingly
Synthesizing your own wild passions by theirs,
Both springing from tragically similar reckless
experimentation.
Day in, day out,
The full loudness – almost quiet – of our mornings
Shifts for the shit-storm
Then back for those seconds we only realize in hindsight;
Never at peace.

Freedom
Ben Kandov

As time passes on, and we feel we feel
Uselessness pass over and over
Over us in the form of a lulling,
Blanket stitched with seams of laziness.
When your aloneness that isn't lonely
Manifests in you bit by bit yourself,
Gnaws into your self-worth subconsciously
And you don't do anything about it.
Study past reflections of memories,
Memories that aren't worth anything,
Actions that should've been acted but haven't,
And won't ever, still, and remember this:
Inevitable future of failure
I think of when I'm lulled to sleep.

About Ben Kandov:

Ben Kandov lives in Queens, New York, where he edits the Hype Journal at Bard Early College. "Freedom" is his first published poem.

About Earphones:

I think I finally understand why so many people are sitting on the bus or subway or strolling around the streets with headphones plugged in their ears. It's not because they actually wanna listen to music, it's because they don't wanna overhear all the asinine conversations bubbling around them.

About Defecating:

Is it a universal instinct to gaze admiringly and proudly into the toilet at the mushy coils, blobs, splatters and nuggets of shit that slide, drop and jump out of the anus every morning? Or is it just me?

Taking it Up the Ass
Mike Algera

In this cosmic coliseum, principle takes it up the ass in this winding gauntlet of occurrence. At work, at school, at the grocery store, at the airport

hey principle, take it up the ass or suck dick! Crawl through the trenches or fly the Mile High.

It seems the omniscient emperor has reversed his definitions. The former was once subterfuge of hope,
hope that was nailed to the ground, now even
the Haitians discard such context

drink more, smoke large nicotine phalluses, reach Friday, hit 5 PM.

By means of occurrence

you're spoiled milk, you're sour grapes, you're the wine that's been corked

well done
corn starched &

goosed.

Dear telemarketing agent
Mike Algera

we represent the do not call list
here is our package deal
surveys say
your life is being held ransom
you cannot save yourself
you are free to lock up your wife and children
as we own their visas
do not attempt escape
we have tapped your cars with plastic explosives
the world stands by
as our eardrum

we are taking back weeknights &
sundays
expect a call round dinnertime

(click)
 ...

About Mike Algera:

MJD Algera is a mid-twenty something approaching thirty, the lightning bug mentioned in passing at a fly by night artist's lounge, a former Ontario scholar, Power of the Pen contest judge, McMaster graduate, advent reader, Blogger and Googler, co-editor and co-publisher of Word Salad, heavyweight performer at the Artword Artbar and champion dog walker. Like him on Facebook. Like his chapbooks, *Outskirts* and *Like Indigenous Tiger*. Like his heroes Johnny Cash, Leonard Cohen, King Kong, Harry Callahan Charles Bukowski and Homer Simpson. Contact him at mikeykillednike2k7@yahoo.ca He would be happy to hear about your poetry and your dog..

An Excerpt from Ernie Lobe's Romantic Journal: On Going Struggles of the Working Man
Rebecca Stone

Every morning,

when my alarm clock squeals at 5:45 AM,

Brenda rolls over and cheerfully whispers in my ear,

"Hon, it's time to get up for work."

Every morning,

when my alarm clock tears me out of my slumber

and my wife rolls over to me and cheerfully says,

"Hon, it's time to get up for work,"

I envision myself ripping the plug out of the wall, wrapping

the black electrical cord around my fist and smashing her big

bucked-teeth down into her pasty pink mouth, screaming,

"I KNOW BITCH! I KNOW!"

Another Excerpt from Ernie Lobe's Romantic Journal
Rebecca Stone

I tell her I'm having a bad day.

A Hemmingway Day

like I feel like cutting myself to let the pain bleed out.

She goes on reading the newspaper.

I sink into a warm bath and stare at her Gillette resting in the

soap dish contemplating suicide for an hour.

But I don't do it,

only because I know it would make her happy.

About Rebecca Stone:

Rebecca Stone is morose, bitter, unattractive both inside and outside, and hates the world more than she hates herself. She writes poetry about Ernie Lobe to stop herself from committing self murder.

Mammogram
Marsha A. Temlock

Inhale
Don't breathe
Don't move.

Fearing fear
Doubting doubt
Await with consternation
The constellation's banded light.
The Milky Way, the galaxy where
a hundred billion spiraling stars,
global clusters, seed the universe
and now these orbs
where once you nursed.
How perverse.

Astronomy. Alchemy. Astrology.
Let's scan the sky
you and I for

  * Aries,
   * Pisces
    * Leo
     * Cancer.

And then forbear another year
Fearing fear
Doubting doubt

Exhale
Breathe
Move on.

The Seltzer Man
Marsha A. Temlock

The last step of the flight of stairs is so steep I have to toe it,
and cling to the banister shivering in grandma's door.
I sidestep a crate of green bottles.
Grandma is blind.
I give her my basket of goodies
Snow White's red cheeked apples
Hansel and Gretel cookies
(Nothing but crumbs).

Grandma gives me a quarter.
Here bubala give this to the seltzer man.
Go Go

The seltzer man has yellow teeth.
His cheeks are hollow.
His lips are wormy.
His bare arms furry.
Three crates on his broad back,
he bounds the steps
    two
      by
        two.

Sets down the crates,
Steals the empties,
Snatches the coin
Sticks out his pink taffy tongue
Farts.

About Marsha Temlock:

Marsha Temlock is the published author of "Your Child's Divorce: What to Expect … What You Can Do," and featured blogger on divorce for the Huffington Post. She is also an adjunct instructor of English at Norwalk Community College in Connecticut, where the kids have been a well-spring of inspiration.

About Civilization:

The foundation of civilization is built upon the expressions of gratitude and remorse. Civilization is saying "Sorry." Civilization is saying "Thank you."

About Obesity:

Obesity shouldn't be rewarded with handicapped parking spaces. Really, fat people should be relegated to the farthest end of the parking lot, and have to walk as far as possible to get into Wal-Mart, you know, for the sake of their heath. If obesity is a disability, anorexia should be one too.

No Refunds
Yevgeniy Levitskiy

Within 7 days,
swap video source for
nourishing cash,
guaranteed refunds
if tested on animals.
See sales tax for
enriching clearance
items
that will tumble dry
when dirty.
Postage-based info uses
mild herbal trimming and will not guide
soothing coupons in any mail box
This last invoice contains
invigorating pro-vitamins,
which will not be accepted
or redeemed if found.
Hydrating rights reserved
by this strip
of post-industrial
mango butter.

SOURCE: Burt's Bees lip balm, Cablevision remote control, Puma t-shirt, Staples coupon, Modell's sporting goods card, Key Food savings card, Kiehl's Tea Tree oil shampoo bottle.

Soften
Yevgeniy Levitskiy

The soften serves two
of the finest types of
luxuries available
for purchase in today's
bullish market. Blue-pink
T-shirts and empty waists
with the scent of Clorox
on them surround the first soften.
Unkept and abused,
the soften is nothing
more than a ruse that
sums up all the reviews
and popular web views. By
watching tongue-tied media
news and hearing ancient
Mississippi blues makes for
some untidy tunes. Nice
cartoons that zoom and bloom
out of soften number two. The
wise attitude of Marxist-quoting
dudes and their platitudes is
beyond social avenues that
present riots to response
to Western values and
downloads, or so I'm
told. I'm ashamed to
say that I live in violent
and backward times,

more or less. I'm ashamed
that I have to pretend
to love those that don't
have my best interests
in heart. Worst of all,
I'm ashamed to
be, just
me.

About Yevgeniy Levitskiy:

Yevgeniy Levitskiy has a B.A. in English-Education from Brooklyn College, and is currently pursuing a M.A. His writing has been published in The Books They Gave Me (Free Press/Simon & Schuster), *The Fiction Shelf*, *Everyday Other Things*, and elsewhere. He is currently at work on a middle-grade novel.

About Personal Hygiene:

It's like, who honestly washes their hands after they piss unless they're in a public bathroom. Yeah, if I'm at the airport, or a restaurant, and someone else is there, I'll soap up for the sake of civilization, but it's only for show, I don't really care if I have ultraviolet traces of urine or feces on my hands. However, if I see some other fucker walk out of the men's without soaping up I'll think he's deranged, borderline psychotic. At least pretend washing your hands matters. You know, for the sake of civilization.

This Is My Status
Steven Mayoff

There are many like it, but this one
is mine. My status is my best friend.
It is my life. I must master it as I must master
my life. My status, without me, is useless.
Without it I am useless.
I will keep my status clean and ready.
We will become part of each other. It is a face
that I present to the world.
It is a beacon by which others may reflect
on my public triumphs and a gateway
through which others may enter
my private fears.
I will eschew privacy as I would an enemy.
My status is a weapon with which I will combat
my loneliness. It is an indelible
stain and a mask
of truth.
Fourteen of my friends like my status.
Six of these friends are people
I have never met. What connects
us all is that we are constantly thinking

about death. We fear that we
will die alone.
My status will live on after my death.
It is my legacy to future generations.
I can write my status
on the head of a pin. It is a speck
in the void. My status
is a constant reminder that I will never
achieve all of my goals. My dreams
will come to nothing.
This knowledge is my only comfort.
This is my status. This is my death.

Motifs
Steven Mayoff

I
Let us improvise motifs on neck
and shoulder, in the small of the back
and behind the knee, running blind fingers
over an accordion's buttons, coaxing
a garlicky wheeze from cracked leather,
a thin current filling the spaces (minute
pockets of eternity).

II
The real music exists between
the notes, a serpentine shimmer disturbs
the air. The clarinet's reed stiffens
to life between saintly lips and confesses
all secret misgivings through a high black bell.
Let us practice etudes on cuticles of keys and soft
pedals, tongues strumming inner strings.

III
The bow glides across tightly-wound tendons,
a loving scrape on an open nerve.
Let us dance beneath a score of crows... ecstasy

**across sky and wire and we two scarecrows, a voicing
of dry grass, hesitation and desire, pushing
the 360-degree periphery, wind-loosened borders
disturbing our air.**

About Steven Mayoff:

Steven Mayoff is a writer living on Prince Edward Island, Canada. His fiction and poetry have appeared in journals across Canada, the USA and in Ireland, Algeria and France. His story collection, *Fatted Calf Blues*, won a 2010 PEI Book Award, was shortlisted for a 2010 ReLit Prize and was a Top 5 Finalist for the 2011 CBC Cross-Country Bookshelf. His novel, *Blessing and Song*, will be published by Bunim & Bannigan Ltd.

Young courtesan
Kevin Thornburgh

She brings him
a white bun
on a white plate
she brings him
a song and
a dance
she brings him
the opera
but she will
not show him
her birthmark
in the early
morning light
of Nanchang

Once
Kevin Thornburgh

Once, I remember, I was watching a
Film in physical anthropology class,
And the native killed the deer and,
In a second, cut him open, and put
Him on a stick: one moment he was
Alive and then the next, dead, on a
Piece of wood. Alas. Poor Yorick, etc.
How delicate is life. But, not delicate,
The spear through the flesh, hard
To pull out, hard to put in, but quick,
Death.

About Kevin Thornburgh:

Kevin Thornburgh earned an MFA at Antioch LA in 2000. He has published four books on Amazon.com: That Lucky Ole Sun; San Gabriel Valley Stories; 11 Meditations or Blue Heron Fishing; and Birdbath poems. He is currently working on a new poetry manuscript which may or may not also include stories. Kevin has published in many poetry magazines such as The Pacific Review, and California Quarterly. He has an interest in Asian poetry and Film as can be seen in some of his recent work.

About What I Wish I Could Say:

Maybe I'm an egomaniac, but I could care less about my friends Facebook photos or any of their photos unless I'm in them.

About Cliches:

This might sound cliché, but whatever, clichés work, clichés make sense, people relate to clichés that's why people always use them. They're effective because they paint familiar pictures. They're good because they make it so people don't have to think too hard. And really, who wants to have to think? Anyway, at the risk of sounding cliché "If it ain't broke, don't fix it."

Runaway Tractor
Larry Schug

Lennon called it instant karma,
the preacher, reaping what you sow,
the judge says actions have consequences,
some simply say shit happens.
The poet says, talk about metaphor
slappin' your face,
kickin' your ass,
shakin' you awake
like your old man waking you for school;
metaphor gushing like wasted maple sap
as the hose lets loose from the tank
of maple nectar, free-flowing from the tap,
the John Deere 2020, headed down the hill,
nobody at the wheel,
and no stoppin' it with prayers or curses,
all because you failed to set the brake,
put the tractor in gear,
chock the wheels, front and rear.

Lesson From a Zen Master
Larry Schug

The radio weather report,
the computer radar display
and the clouds moving in from the west
all signal heavy rain, lightning and thunder.
The cat knows this as well as I do,
though from sources I'm not privy to;
yet he sleeps with his head on the window sill,
unconcerned.
The cat, a master practitioner of Zen,
lives in the present,
while I fret about trees falling on the house
and working in the rain tomorrow.

About Larry Schug:

Larry Schug is happily retired from a life of physical labor. He's published six books of poems and is a past Loft-McKnight Fellowhip winner and a two-time Pushcart Prize nominee. He lives in St. Wendell Twp., Minnesota with wife, dog and cats and volunteers at a local college writing center.

TIMELESS RESONANCE
Sylvester Pilgrim

I love it when you come
It's wet and wild
Luminous and warm, sometimes…cooler
But always it's loud and forceful
The way you lather my back
Makes me shiver with anticipation
I languish in your embrace
Your cling is strong, your scent…intoxicating
There are complaints,
But I don't care,
They have no appreciation for your beauty
Your twisted marvels embrace my serenity
I long to see your forked flares ignite my pastures
And dance across my meadow
Hear your fire and flourish in your rumble
When you leave, my petals drip from your charisma
And in the distance, your echo reverberates in my soul

PEERLESS LUCIDITY
Sylvester Pilgrim

In my depths of solitude
I stand at the precipice
Gaping into the maw of the abyss
Filament strings of what could be
Taunt me with wanton promises
But beneath the ebon glade
I see the lurking of rue
The magenta sirens that repulse my yearning
And prolong my perch
Locked in an endless battle
Neither conqueror nor vanquished
The eternal struggle
That is the landscape of my mind

About Sylvester Pilgrim:

Sylvester Pilgrim is an aspiring author and poet who currently lives in Toronto, Canada. As well as writing, he is also a photographer and performs in community theatre with a brief appearance and voice over in a short film. He has had previous publications for short stories as well as poetry. In addition, he has won first prize in the Seneca Colleges Salon's third annual creative writing contest in the area of short fiction. You can read more of his work at: sylvesterpilgrim.wordpress.com.

Guitar Man
Rebecca Halton

Humming & strumming
His old guitar;
He serenades the passersby.
Condescending copper bullets,
Crowded corners,
Knowing,
Judging,
Bloodshot eyes.
One hand raised,
His eyes alight,
A smile begins to crack.
Cigarette ashes
Fall to the ground,
As I smile,
And I wave back.

Joggers
Rebecca Halton

I think you are wrong
I think you are running
Denying what even you
Have claimed to be possible
And now I understand
My problem is I am not.
I have been stationary for years,
Watching the world
Thank you for teaching me
To love and accept
That we're all just
Pretentious joggers.

About Rebecca Halton:

Rebecca Michelle Halton, better known as Becky, is a creative soul; neurotically trapped in the passive- aggressive body of an aspiring student-writer. Becky's work seeks to connect with others in encouraging a message of acceptance, by openly exploring life's challenges and appreciating the simplistic beauty in nature, love and solitude. Currently residing in Ottawa, ON, Canada, she is in her final year at Carleton University as a Psychology and English student. In her spare time, Becky enjoys writing poetry and short-stories, making cards, scrapbooking, painting, designing photo frames and indulging in the creative arts.

About How to tell the difference between Art and Entertainment:

Art evokes thought, entertainment distracts thought.

About Technology:

Our constant, perhaps even excessive interactions with machines are causing the disintegration of human conscience. When you grow up in a world where your best friends run on batteries and nearly every hobby you have requires electricity and an on-switch, it makes sense that all these experiences shared with conscienceless, indifferent machines, would in some way impair your ability to empathize. The more we interact with machines, the more we will behave like them.

Cast Light
Mike Thorn

Dregs of incense slither through 60 watts of light.
She passes the roach so he can scorch his diaphragm.
Quasi-fictional flashbacks take arachnid forms,
confessions swimming in smoke …
Let's fuck in the park she says.
It's too cold he says.
Sacramental figures adorn the wall,
wraiths in waning white hue …
It's time to change the light bulb but she likes being
frightened.
Paradise lost in chronic self-glory,
threads of smoke that drift above the sin.
Intercourse deflates his pupils.
I'm sorry God he thinks as she extends the lighter.
Here come on try it—it makes you feel alive she says.
All he wants is to write the novel
but only poems will come.

15ᵗʰ Ave Funeral
Mike Thorn

Here come the dope-fogged morning sounds—
the wrong RPM setting for
living room finger traps:
scratched records, butter-slimed dishes,
pot resin and foil bags.
Watch eusociality as a mural in motion—
six biramous legs bicycling air,
antennae and mandibles
pecking at the exoskeleton.
You exit with a shudder.
You buy some Advil.
You rub your eyes and frame the event with acronyms.

About Mike Thorn:

Mike is studying English at Mount Royal University in Calgary. His work has most recently been published in STOPGap magazine and in the book *Sleep & Ecstasy* (co-written by Tomas Boudreau). He has appeared in a number of films, including Brendan Prost's *Choch* and *Generation* Why. Mike also wrote, co-directed and starred in the independent film *The Coldest Months*.

Love, Life, and other Games Lost
Jacob Nantz

I crafted the art of
Love in the Moment,
Knew just the way to grip her back
And make her feel like it was real,
Spoke whispers that sounded scripted because they were;
I had a way of making foreign sheets feel familiar
And convincing her into connections
That I held high, stretched until they stiffened
like a rope tugging too much weight,
then I would watch it snap and shatter
what hung below, splatter into
something for which I felt nothing
only because I wouldn't let myself watch,
or listen.
He told me in a tavern that night
That he had never been loved,
And I laughed at his lament
Of such a silly thing,
And he laughed at my taunting
pretending he agreed,
And though his cries I did not hear,
this rope did not snap,
And I wish it had,
like every other thing that ever loved me,
When I saw him swaying from
The creaking rafters in the morning

Answers found on a Café Corner near Oriel College
Jacob Nantz

Around my eighth pint
I began to make personal observations
That were far from profound,
Pondered life's subtleties and enjoyed the peaceful
Shade that hid me from the sun.
I've often wondered why the woman's
Voice on my navigation system
Has a British accent.
Maybe research showed people are most comforted by the dialect—
It is much more soothing than a Midwest nasal slur.
It does possess more class than a southern twang,
(though I've always thought the sound of the south to be sexy)
But why British?
Why a woman?
I'm an American man for God's sake.
And the waitress interrupted with the bill,
Somehow soothing my frustration with her voice.
I left her a hefty tip and stumbled back to my dorm
Under the guidance of the Oxford towers.

About Jacob Nantz:

Jacob Nantz teaches high school English in the Chicago suburbs. He received his degree in English Education from Northern Illinois University in 2009. Nantz hosts weekly poetry workshops with his students, and works with the Young Chicago Authors organization through an outreach program in Aurora, Illinois. He also participates in the Uptown Poetry slam on Sunday nights at the Green Mill in Chicago.

SHADES OF TIME
Katherine Givens

Loosen the ties
of the desire
for a dead memory.
Attempting
to revive
what is lost
in the shades of time
will lead
to a conflict of wills.
Since Fate
is the opponent,
one is destined
for defeat.
Allow
the veins of life
to guide
the future.
Do not battle
the shades of time
for the sake
of a memory.

HIDDEN BEAUTY
Katherine Givens

A calm front
can fool the world.
A wise mind
can look deeper.
With a little observation,
one can learn
that under a façade
meant to mask the soul
is a torrent of emotions
bottled inside
a loving heart.
The shame is
the world will never
understand the depth
of this soul
due to the stings
life has served.
The only window
to peer through
is the scribbling and jottings
of creativity.

About Katherine Givens:

Katherine Givens is a college student but a writer at heart. Her fiction has appeared in *The Copperfield Review* and *The Enchanted File Cabinet*. Her poetry has been in many magazines, including *Nazar Look, Literary Juice, Apollo's Lyre,* and *BareBack Magazine*.

Buntings
Jason Barry

Father told me once to
be a man

for I was not meant to sketch
a daffodil or chase the buntings

as they swooped like paper planes
from our red chimney

flight lines of curlicues and
feathers

don't just sit there
he'd say on Sunday mornings

fishing rods in hand
but I'd grin and let my feet

dangle down into the water
toes tickled by the skins

of passing trout
when I was eight years old

I learned what all sons know
Uncle Bill's daughter in our garage

if you mention this to anyone
I'll destroy you, Dad said

grey hands like shattered clay on
a child's breast

we walked into to the study
that autumn evening

sunset painted above the lake
I remember him whispering that

these suckers pack a heavy punch
twenty hollow-points in a plastic box

    pro casing
    heart crushing
    silver feeling

he placed a shell in my jacket pocket
kissed my forehead lightly

and said to play in the field
out back with Jenny

Remembering Francisco
Jason Barry

In the secluded shade under leafy Banyan trees, stood a house with stony walls and thin wisps of ivy. Garnished inside with vibrant paintings of pineapple, bird nests, and poppies, this was the home of Francisco Espinosa, the casa of the wise one.

I recall a summer's visit when he clenched me by the waist and whispered tales of the old city — of evenings spent hunting barefoot for crawdads in the shallow tide of the *Malecón*, his little hands grasping slimy tales and tossing them one by one into a silver bucket.

Francisco called to mind the image of a sacred crucifix he'd received at Confirmation, the one he later traded to his cousin Rita for a glass of *jugo de cana* and a backpack full of sweet corn.

Stories were told of the young man in Havana: A handsome youth who had sheepishly written stanzas with paint brushes made of horse hair and dried honeysuckle, and drafted poems on the stationary his father sent home from journeys to Venice and Madrid (the timelessly elegant folios with a pair of blooming primrose etched on every corner).

Intoxicated that night we met on aged rum and Sherry, sweat pooled in his palms as he spoke of infidelity with his wife of thirty years, the woman who'd passed away the month before. In 1959, he told me, they danced together on a marble veranda to a German cabaret, her in cashmere and heels, and he in a striped tuxedo.

When the event was over they drove back though strands of hail, cuddled and cozy in the leather seat of a Plymouth taxi cab. Yes, there are some things we can never forget, even when we want to. With his arms draped upon my shoulders and his eyes fixed on the stars, he mentioned that time elapses but memory remains active in dreams.

We will always be as close as then, he said, letting me go with a kiss.

About Jason Barry:

Jason Barry is based in Boulder, Colorado. He is the poetry editor at The Bacon Review, and acquisitions editor for books in philosophy at Paradigm Publishers. His recent work has appeared in The Citron Review, Fat City Review, BarebackLit, On a Junket, and CU Independent. He is currently at work on a collaborative project with the multimedia Brazilian artist, Marcos Serra, entitled: "Poetry in Motion: Words, Concepts, and Abstraction," which will be presented in Los Angeles in 2013.

About Immortality:

Humanity created an afterlife, not because we felt we needed a reward or a punishment, or because we needed something to believe in, but because, more than anything else, we desire to live. Morality ensures this. As long as everyone follows the rules, everyone will have a greater chance of survival. But because we hate to be ruled by men, God was invented to enforce the rules. Fame was created to make us think we'll actually live forever.

About Gender Equality:

Like, if men and women are truly equal, the same and all that, women would be showing up at playgrounds and train stations ripping open trench coats exposing themselves. Really, there should be more female flashers. It's not fair.

iWorld
Donna Hawks

Granite egos sparkling like renovated countertops
Hiding/concealing the painful truth locked inside
To split their atoms would create honesty
To separate them would cause havoc within themselves

The insecure are polite
The egotistical are too jaded and pissed off to be polite.

But we all hide behind the **i**
                      Phone
                      Pad
                      Pod

Don't
look at me
talk to me
ask me anything

Can't you see **i**

               'M IMORTANT
               HAVE FRIEDNS,

               A SOCIAL LIFE

They're here
in the palm of my gluey hand.
An entire iWorld waiting for ME, ME, ME.

One Night Stand
Donna Hawks

She wakes up
the distinct taste of penis on her tongue
Metallic urine and sugar free saltines
that's what penises taste like, you know.
But whose cock did she eat last night?
The Stoli is all she remembers.
Frantically, hair tangled, make-up smudged, she sifts
through the trash desperately searching for a Trojan
The possibility of a fetus cooking in her womb doesn't
worry her
that can be taken care of ~ discarded.
But the acronyms,
Those are keepers ~ those are fear.
The basket next to the bed is empty
'cept for lipstick stained cigarette butts and an old
eyeliner pencil.
There is no cummy coagulated Kleenex
No condom wrapper
Panic quickens her pulse,
and she prays,
I just hope I swallowed.

About Donna Hawks:

Donna Hawks, AKA Tim Giffy, lives with her partner and two cats. Poetry is her passion, but she works at a Taco Bell to pay the rent.

Horology
Sebastiaan Bonnarens

24:00 A man, lying dead in the street.

23:00 A man, getting stabbed in his chest.

22:00 A man, refusing to give his money.

21:00 A man, threatened by a 17 year old criminal.

20:00 A man, on his way to his homely loneliness.

19:00 A man, coming out the doorway of a Tobacconist.

18:00 A man, buying a pack of cigarettes.

17:00 A man, entering a tobacconist and is greeted with a welcoming "Told you so".

16:00 A man, tearing off his nicotine patch and throwing his gum away.

15:00 A man, thinking "what's the point."

14:00 A man, putting his cell phone away.

13:00 A man, saying that he just wants to go home.

12:00 A man, being told that he should come, that it would help.

11:00 A man, explaining what happened.

10:00 A man, being asked why he isn't at the stop smoking meeting.

09:00 A man, receiving a phone call.

08:00 A man, getting up, trying to stay strong.

07:00 A man, dropping on his knees, trying to fight the flood in his eyes.

06:00 A man, walking aimlessly.

05:00 A man, wondering what he should do now

04:00 A man, seeing the ambulance drive away.

03:00 A man, calling a hospital.

02:00 A man, crying.

01:00 A woman, lying dead in the street.

A Strange Witness
Sebastiaan Bonnarens

Sun passes by, shadows reform,

A man tormented by his remorse,

For long ago, it hit him hard,

A duck foresaw his own demise,

As it was witness to what he'd done,

The duck for one, had to die.

About Sebastiaan Bonnarens:

The name was Sebastian, a name of kings, of rulers, of Caesars, given to a boy who can't even rule his own thoughts. His mind always seemed to fight him, the sea in his brain never tranquil. But he fought on and he still does, trying his hardest to make himself function in today's complicated world. His shield is his mask that he crafts so delicate and wears so easily, hiding himself from the unknown. His sword is the machine that contains all he holds dear, an advanced file cabinet answering to all his whims.

Chelsea Morning
Brendan Sullivan

Morning tea comes too soon
with a slap of newsprint
at my door while twenty floors below

some sweet young thing
promises the end of the world
on a postcard.
If these walls could talk
I would probably weep
because the paint
has not been seen in years
and covers nothing.

My pillow is a thin buffer
against the noise next door,
and down the hall
I can hear the maid
flick her ashes
down the laundry chute,
slipping the matches
into her bra
and praying the guy in 113
did not dream of her again
all over his sheets.

My blanket weighs a ton
and the elevator grinding
to a halt
is my last stab
at anything rational.

This must be how Joey felt
or maybe Sid.
You know -
funky in a beat up sort of way,
the mattress upstairs
chugging away
and last night
taking up too much space
in my mouth.

river
Brendan Sullivan

cold punches through the river,
webbed silver trails leading down
down to the caves
where we lost the children last summer.
buttons left roaming in the rocks
cleave the past in two,
their tiny holes gaping through
tender fiddle ferns
and the cry of white geese
mocking us like snow.

the tide claimed their faces,
rude shallows pulling them down
down to the bottom
where the wet could not reach them.
skin caught like cloth in silt
carves the riverbed,
the slender reeds wrapping round
knots of slippery elm
and the glimpse of dank weeds
marking us like ash.

our hands try to remember
how they felt
when we put them to bed that last time,

the soft flannel of their good nights
bunched in our arms like angels,
never dreaming
their toys would wake up alone

or that god would forget
where we live.

About Brendan Sullivan:

Brendan is a lifelong beach bum who has turned from acting to poetry, as he finds it a more remarkable muse. When not chasing his muse, he also enjoys surfing, sailing and diving. He turns to the ocean for inspiration, solace and sanity. His work has been published at Wordsmiths, The Missing Slate, Every Writer's Resource, Gutter Eloquence, A Sharp Piece of Awesome, After Tournier, Bareback Magazine and Bare Hands.

All Beauty
Keith Kennedy

Projection
Everything I am, cast into all I see
Rocks into water
Absorption
It's about me, it contains me, it reflects me, echoes me
It is a beautiful painting for I am willing to be beautiful
It is a song of legend for I am able to hear it
It is a word among words, for I may repeat this word at my leisure.

I resonate – added to all of it as if born within it
I love it all for it all loves me
I am a perfect life cycle
I am bent inward
I exude, yet remain introverted
I take, yet remain giving
I am all beauty.

With boots on – naked in the woods besides
Keith Kennedy

I am an out of focus picture of you
No lines – but clouds of shadow play
No arms risen – just rockets of visible sound rising
No being – just endings, and faded treks into way away sunlight
No being – just endings, and blurry goodbye-ing over the horizon

I am holding an out of focus picture of myself
You are clear – as light beneath the water's surface

About Keith Kennedy:

Keith Kennedy is a writer of things and a joker of jokes. He's been nominated for the Pushcart Prize and the Rhysling Award, recently appearing as Himself w/Beard in various places. Check out his daily dealings at www.askkeithanything.blogspot.com.

About Friendship:

This kinda makes feel like a bitch to say, but others peoples pain gives me pleasure, like I'm happy that my friend R~~~~~ is 34, has no boyfriend, and probably won't ever get married. It makes me happy that my other friend J~~~~ is putting on weight as she ages and is losing her looks. I don't know why, but other peoples misery makes me happy. Well, not everybody, just the people I know, who I'm in this totally silent life competition with. Not like, the poor people in Swaziland who have a 31 year life expectancy, just my friends.

About Wishes:

Sometimes I wish I was a seagull just so I could drop shit on people's heads and not get in any trouble.

e.q.

highs
Robert Swereda

And dry
And low
And mighty
As a kite

Beam *blood pressure* brass cal church comedy commands commission country court days explosive fashion fidelity frequency *gain antennae* gears german ground heels holiday horse hurdles jinks jumping life marking masses noon places point priesthood profile relief renaissance
Road rollers school seas season sign society spot street style table tea tech tides time treason water wires

Altitude cerebral oedema
Back binding
Class Concept Count
definition television
Density lipoproteins
Employment deficit
End energy five flown flyers grade handedness *hat cymbals* level
Level languages
Level waste
Lows maintenance mindedness muck-a-muck octane performance pitches powered pressure ranking rent resolution rises risk sounding speed spirited stakes stick strung *temperature superconductor* tension test toned top ups value voltage *water mark*

Ball balling balls binder born boy bred brow chair criticism education law learning mathematics jack land life lighted tail way

subs
Robert Swereda

Acidly Adar Aerial Alpine Alternate Antarctic Apical Aquatic Arachnoids Atomic Audition Base Calibre Celestial Cellular Class Clinical Committee Conscious Compact Continent Contract Cortex Cortical Culture Deacon Diaconal Directories Divide Division Dominant Duct Due Edit Equatorial Erin Families Field Floor Fossil Frame Genera Genus Grades Group Gum Head Human Imago Irrigate Join Judice Kingdom Lease Let Lieutenant Lime Lingual Literature *Machine gun* Marginal Marine Merge Microscopic *Miniature camera* Mission Multiple Normality Notebook Orbital Order Ordinary Oscine Oxide Pena Plot Polar *Post office* Ring Rosa Routine Saharan Scribe Script Section Sequence Sere Serve Set Shell Shrub Side Sister Social Soil Solar Song Sonic Species Specific Stage Stance Standard Station Strata Stratosphere Structural Tangent Tenancy Tending Terminal Text Tidal Title Total Tract Traction Tropical Umbrella Unit Urbanized Version Viral Vocalized Way Woofer Zero

About Robert Swereda:

Robert Swereda is a member of the Filling Station collective in Calgary. He studied creative writing at Capilano University in Vancouver. Recent work has been published in *In Air/Air Out, Steel Bananas*, *CV2*, *The Enpipe Line Anthology* and *Poetry Is Dead*.

What I Can't Say
Rebecca Rose Taylor

Why is it that the words I want to say most
The ones that should be so easy do not come
That I am afraid of picking up a pen or a phone and telling you
Two little words like you matter
Or maybe even, let's have coffee
At night in my dreams it is so easy
But in the daylight, fear or common sense take over
And I agonize about what I want to say
But cannot seem to find a way
My emotions sway back and forth
And I don't know how to bridge the gap
My heart wants to say the words
But my brain won't let it
This is why the words I want to say
Remain unspoken.

Recalculating
Rebecca Rose Taylor

Life is like a GPS system
Recalculating each car's path
My heart wishes it could be that steady
But it waivers like a roadblock
Wishing you were here
But knowing that the map took you elsewhere
My brain tries to reconnect our paths
But timing stalls our rebuild
For now our street is closed
Life's roadwork will persist.

About Rebecca Rose Taylor:

Rebecca Rose Taylor has loved inventing stories since before she could write them down. Some of her previous publications include Barebacklit, Perspectives Magazine, Long Story Short and The Toronto Small Press Group. She works full time as the administrative assistant – finance & reception at a senior's home where she has the opportunity to meet many people. When Rebecca isn't working, writing or reading, she enjoys helping on the family farm, knitting, crocheting and quilting..

About Getting Intoxicated:

There are few reasons to pollute oneself with the myriad narcotics and spirits available to the general public. One is to celebrate. Another is to mask the pangs of existence. I pollute myself to celebrate masking the pangs of existence.

About Antisocialism:

Maybe it's just me, but sports are better to watch on TV. Recorded music is superior to live shows. And I'd rather view art online than go to a museum.

When names held power
Alyssa Cooper

Past the point
of pain,
we've reached uncertainty;
waking up wrong
and confused,
I've misplaced something,
something unspeakably
important,

but I don't know what.

I wake up groggy,
out of focus,
and I know that something
is wrong.
Something
is not the way that we remember.
Rooms are still,
and air
is thin;
something elemental was changed
when we weren't looking.

I wake up missing

something;

I wake up with your name
on my lips.

The Pen
Alyssa Cooper

My words flow freer
from a pen.
My mind is muddled
by circuitry
and keys.
My thoughts freeze -

but the pen
is conduit.
It draws out
the poison
inside me;
infuses it
with something beautiful.

About Alyssa Cooper:

Alyssa Cooper was born in Belleville Ontario, and has lived in Canada for her entire life. After spending two years studying Fine Arts at York University, she left Toronto to pursue an education in Graphic Design. Her work has been featured in poetry anthologies and literary magazines. Her first novel, Salvation, is anticipated for release from Melange Books in fall 2012, and her novella, Sunshine, is available now from Fiction Lake. She is currently attending college in Oshawa, where she lives with her typewriter and her personal library.

Fireside
Sandra Langer

You opened a door
put a candle in the window
as bright as your thoughtful smiling face
your sharp blue eyes shinning
under wonderful fly away silver bright hair

You make me faint blinking in the light
your breasts like fully rounded orbs
rose gold moonlight
reveal themselves shifting
pink and rose delight
your budding passion unfurling petals welcoming
pure rainbow pleasures
husky whispers warm as a fireside
making everything right

Brains and boobs delirious with joy
voices quivering with relief
feeling our distinct ways through
these new beginnings
navigating the emotional mind fields
darting through the picket fences
all the while
exchanging smoldering looks
shooting knowing glances
body parts gripped
with convulsive satisfaction

Knowing each other's trigger points
faces flushed
dissolving into each other's touches
hot waves sweeping through blood
inflamed by desire

Kissing softly, roughly, teasingly, deeply
mouthing breathless words of desire
Here, There, Everywhere
fluid running down each other's tongues
throats, thighs
legs sprawled
completely ourselves in naked bliss

Killer
Sandra Langer

Undiluted moonlight-
beguiles, enchants and deceives
the dark side of the moon
only comes into view as it turns away.

How it works its magic on our imagination.
Rim of the harvest moon
cutting its way into the sky
swollen spellbinding orb of silver light pooling in the dark.

Alcohol the lubricant of genius
Encircle with a corona
mirrored in the hexagonal reflections
of falling snow crystals
firing glints of purple light.

A shot of moonshine in a glass
shooting bright lights
the amber waters fogging the brain.
Nothing to prevent it all from slipping away entirely.

About Sandra Langer:

Cassandra Langer is an art critic, artist/poet living in Jackson Heights, New York. She is the author of seven books including her forthcoming critical biography of the American expatriate lesbian painter Romaine Brooks entitled *All or Nothing: The Many Masks of Romaine Brooks (1874-1970)* (University of Wisconsin Press -2013). Her art and poetry are a distinctive blend of classical metaphor, personal mythology, sensuousness and loss. Poets who have inspired her include: Basho, Baudelaire, Cavafy, Dickenson, Elytis, Mallarme, Pound, Rambeau, Rich and Whitman.

About Depression:

What's the point of crying if there isn't an audience to gain sympathy from?

My Crazed Mind
Melissa June

My troubling thoughts are tangled
deep inside, within my mind
my sanity wants them strangled
unconscious, eyes blind

A crazed mind, to never think
these manic thoughts
the imagined and reality, never to link
kept entangled within knots

Lost oxygen, a mangled brain
mental pictures blood stained
contemplated ideas I restrain
disturbing thoughts, tightly chained

Thoughts from mind, never divisible
the controlling voices slain
the truth remains invisible
never knowing, I was mentally insane.

My Minds Maze
Melissa June

Rusted gears no longer turning apace
neurons slowly transmitting signals within
though millions of impulses interlace
a current trapped, in a continuous spin

Memories, emotions and thoughts
never received, a conscious lost in circulation
my muscles distorted, left in knots
for impulses have yet to find their destination

Lifeless circuits stand still within my head
as blank eyes lock into a gaze
comatose, turning brain dead
awaiting a flow, through my minds maze.

About Melissa June:

Melissa June is a twenty five year old poetess from Windsor Ontario, who has always had a passion for writing. In some of her poems she writes about crazed thoughts, fantasy creatures, depression, love and nature to name a few. Her dreams are to one day publish a poetry book and being a mother of three beautiful girls she hopes to touch more upon children's poems and to create children's rhyming books.

happy town
Kellen Davis

in happy town(where
the flowers are laughing
&
the birds are singing)
love swims through the air
(we're all
happily soaked)
joy breathes from the trees
(:umbrage of
smiles:)
happiness floats in the pond
(((ripples)carry)laughter)

everyone
is welcome in
happy town
(strange
rs
&
new
comers)

happy town
is a secret paradise
(everyone
knows where it is)
there's a map in your heart
(i found my way there)
&
now
i live in happy town
(im happy)

never-never
Kellen Davis

everyone who isnt(those
who hold their pillow
tight)dreaming
have lost hope(some
where
in the
forest of never-never
outside the castle
in the sky-
baked inside a single
special pie)

the
flickering
flame of faith(the only
guiding light in this
wondrous phantasm)
is sparked by only one thing-
the smile of a happy face

go!with
fIRE and HAsTE
slay the cynical chimera-
lay it to waste!

About Kellen Davis:

Kellen DaKellen Davis is a young, proud Texan who calls Houston his home. His love for poetry finally came to light after taking an upper level English course at Texas State University, where he subsequently basked in the cryptic, iconoclastic musings of e.e. Cummings. Before this 'poetic epiphany and renaissance', he knew little, if not absolutely nothing, about poetry. On the other hand, after this inexplicable revelation, he consumed himself in the poetic art with such fervor, with such a manic embrace, that he was teeter tattering on the borderline of a torrid new passion, and a complete social withdrawal brought about by obsession.

I WORK FOR YOU WITH MY NEUROTIC MIND
Sam Silva

I work for you with my neurotic mind
except to spend the gorgeous hours
in art with all its nature
in the concave of our love.
A plan made real by death
and yet too difficult to be designed
beyond the chaos of the trees and flowers
where fate unravels panting breath
whose sexual sighs reveal their powers
and make for you a painting
near the blanket where we dined.
I love this life
where chaos lifts us up
enough to gaze upon your beauty
in the million ways we work and cry
and drink and love and sup.

COMPUTER POETRY TILL MORNING
Sam Silva

Fatigue come the night, come deep
...a burning fatigue too tired to sleep!
Instead of this thoughts wander off,
kick the sheets and start to cough
smoke and weep and pace the floor
sense the creaking of the door
and chase those flickerings of light
within that deep fatigue of night.

About Sam Silva:

Sam Silva has poetry in several print magazines. For the Past four years his magazine portfolio has grown by and large online including Rio Del Arts, Megaera, Big Bridge, Views unplugged, Comrade Magazine, Ken Again and at least thirty others. Over the years four small presses have published a total of nine chapbooks by Sam Silva for pushcart...these, being Third Lung Press, M.A.F. Press, Alpha Beat Press, Trouth Creek Press. Brown and Yale Universities solicited many of these chapbooks for their libraries.

Tourists
Ted Bussy

She finds life lurking in this smutty back alley in Bangkok
despicable
I find it exhilarating
I feel home
Shall I surrender my swivel chair and cubical,
hand in my nameplate and tie,
enter the domain of a pockmarked whore?
What will I find?
Will I find love?
Will I love what I find?
I'm scared, she says.
I'm alive, I think.
It smells,
stale pussies and sour penises,
poverty and human will.
Why did you bring me here?
To see the show.
To show you to see,
An old man haggling over the price of vagina.
Another bartering for the cost of Viagra.
I'm scared,
I don't care,
Where are we going?
The show,
I know,
But where?
There,
to the end of this smutty back alley in Bangkok,
where despicable lives lurk, with me, wishing I was truly, truly among them.

GIFT
Ted Bussy

We dance naked,
twirling like drunken ballerinas.
She talks too much tonight,
So do I.
She leaves her shit in the toilet the next morning,
It smells like mine, only worse.

About Ted Bussy:

Ted Bussy is a bi-sexual escort from the greater Chicago area. He enjoys lap dances, Exotic birds and silent Russian films. In his spare time he writes erotic poetry and gay lit.

About Labels:

I like putting labels on things, people, ideas, beliefs. Yeah, I know a lot of people don't like to be categorized or have a label slapped on them like a soup can, but it makes me feel more comfortable. Plus, like, labels have the coolest sounding words, especially "ist" words. Artist, environmentalist, philanthropist, existentialist ~ that's a really cool sounding word. But "ic" and "ict" words are usually negative, schizophrenic, psychotic, alcoholic, addict. Even still, call me whatever you want. Brand me! Just try to make it an "ist" word.

About Masturbation:

Does jerking off make you gay? 'Cause if you think about it, it seems pretty gay.

Blue-Collar Twister
Sonnet Mondal

Sweat tries to swim upwards through the hairs
of a labourer building the statue of the herald
but fails and falls in the soil sucked up by heat,
Vanishes as a struggling animal in quicksand;
Dreams drain and entity turns into fossils as slippers
walk over it.
His weapons are a chisel and spade;
He lifts them to protest but vacuum wailing in the curves
of his muscles make it fall again on the mummified ground;
just to dig, dig the ground for
the Herald's statue must stand firm
or his existence will be buried under its
falling weight.
Toils will evaporate with the smile of the moon
The dawn will hear sounds again-
sounds of iron striking against rocks.
The air waits to weave those sounds
and strike a twister with them-
Tall enough for the world to see
bold enough to step over mountains
Clear enough to show the waving hands
begging a day out of slavery.

Reddened Sky
Sonnet Mondal

Trying to track a beam in a moonless night
I find the reddened sky screaming with thunders
in a distant patch over skyscrapers and towers.
Struck by fumes the blood seems to clot
with the dark-red end flaring all over.
Still people have time to look above
and the mill owners must not smile for
we love the skies and we vote out rulers.
The umbrella above is burning and we desire
no collapse but a healing of nature and eyes,
which still gaze above after dinner in new moon nights
for rays of guidance and in full moon nights
to name new constellations rather than
wait to see guiltless quietude crucified
without dissent and voices.
I and with me a million, wishes the life above
to be same; there must be something
away from the life above, just to provide
us a balm of spirituality and profoundness.

About Sonnet Mondal:

Sonnet Mondal is an award winning poet and the founder of *The Enchanting Verses Literary Review.* He has authored eight collections of poetry. His works have appeared in several international literary publications including *The Sheepshead Review (University of Wisconsin, Green Bay), The Penguin Review* (Youngstown State University), *Two Thirds North* (Stockholm University), *California State Poetry Quarterly* (California State Poetry Society) and *Friction Magazine* (New Castle University) to name a few. Most recently, he has been enlisted as a National Record Holder as *"The First Indian to write a new type of Sonnet Poetry"* at the Indian Book of Records.

Dismantle
Maria Emmanuelle Arnidou

This bunch of gears and cogs and screw-ups,

burned chips and overheated parts

silicon core instead of carbon

and malfunctioned CPU

Dismantle it

with every touch and glance and breath of you

Dismount my mecha puppet figure

relieve me of the strings attached

make me a real girl, give me a heart that can be crushed

and mortal skin of clay that can be touched and cut and age

for I fear not the human certainty of death or bloodshed

but I resent this android fate of shutting down -

-not having backup of emotions nor sense of tears flowing down

Disassemble me

I made the start, I broke my winder

I overrode my rigid programming of zero-one

help me to stretch my limited horizon wider

erase my former data one by one

Dismantle it

this rusty structure that cannot decay

Please don't delay

Provide me with a vessel I can call a shrine

of soul

able to die outlived by love's mysterious lullaby

Dismantle me

and leave me lying here alive

Your Light
Maria Emmanuelle Arnidou

You've got it all - all seven colours of the Iris
and yet you feel as if you were the darkest,
loneliest cloud after the heavy rain
the one whose tears have gone in vain
amidst the heavy storm and clash of thunder
You never took a blink of time to wonder
why all the ships at sea gather around you
the reason why you have been seeked by cocky captains,
humble sailors and petty mermaids through the darkest nights
My dear, it's all a matter of your vivid light.
Your faulty thought might be that you descent from darkest
deeds of past that should be punished,
indeed you took a horrid tour of hell
through lifstream's draughts - as most of us
but you came back like all the saints
 who were at first in deep of sin
the difference is, your troubled soul was by default as clean
as drops of dew in the morning of the Seventh Day.
None can deny of being mere fancy dolls of clay, but it's the
ornament within that counts, or its absence
Yours, holds inside a piece of sky,

its milky blue with velvet coloured love

and in this little fragment blue lies magically encompassed

the whole of sun - the rays, the warmth, the shine of life,

because you see, My Dear, it's all a matter of your vivid light.

About Maria Arnidou:

Maria Emmanuelle Arnidou was born in 1984 in Athens, Greece. She studied Sociology at Panteion University of Athens. She has been writing sporadically, mostly poetry, since school years, but only devoted herself in this form of expression after her father's death in 2007, finding solace and refuge in words. Her main influences come from art, music and literature, including creators such as Monet, Gyzis, Mozart, Francoise Sagan, E. A. Poe, K. P. Kavafis, Yannis Ritsos and Odysseas Elytis. She is currently working with her family in setting up a handmade jewelry brand by day and writing by night.

THE POLITICS OF DEATH
Poppy Taylor

Stand to attention.
Initiate your limitation of power
into silhouette.
Take the currency - why taunt
the threat.
You are never going to flay
all those; who stand in your way

Abide by the rules, don't ricochet
A pea in a tin can, is not greatly a man.
Tone down the capacity of your over
stuffed head,
carnage confuses the order of death.

Think you're a power house -
when, just a man of self-worth
That blessed is your name, six|
foot in the grave.
Illuminated sidewalks dance to the beat
Read the headlines - loser!

Cry Me A Daddy...
Poppy Taylor

Burnt fingers forbidden fruit
A surfeit of overripe indulgence.
Torn clean from the bough.
Subterranean ruse masks the gathering of tongues.
Small shards of sweetness
honeyed with a barb.
Papas coming *home* Jack Daniels single malt.
Drained glass; dribbling volatile and ice.
Brittle sick; flavoured smoky bacon crisps.
Spent cache of roll–your-own cigs.
Rivulets of urine apocalyptic flow.
Attractive to your touch -
breast and nipple moulded into
form.
May some man *soon* expose such shabby shame.
Of those poor broken souls worn proud upon your feet.

About Poppy Taylor:

Poppy Taylor is a single female residing in Cumbria England. She has two real passions in her life. They are her writing and the animals she shares her 4 acres small holding with. She fills her days feeding her several dogs, numerous cats, and 3 pet sheep as well as any stray wildlife that happens to be passing by. When not busy writing or looking after the 4 legged pet brigade, she enjoys nothing better than pottering around car boots sales looking to bag that elusive lost forgotten antique.

Picfecturing Spontaneity
Darren Simon

She snaps our picture
Then again,
again, again, and again.
Wait, one more time!
Is this a movie?
It can't be REAL LIFE.
She had a hair out of place.

Language Arts
Darren Simon

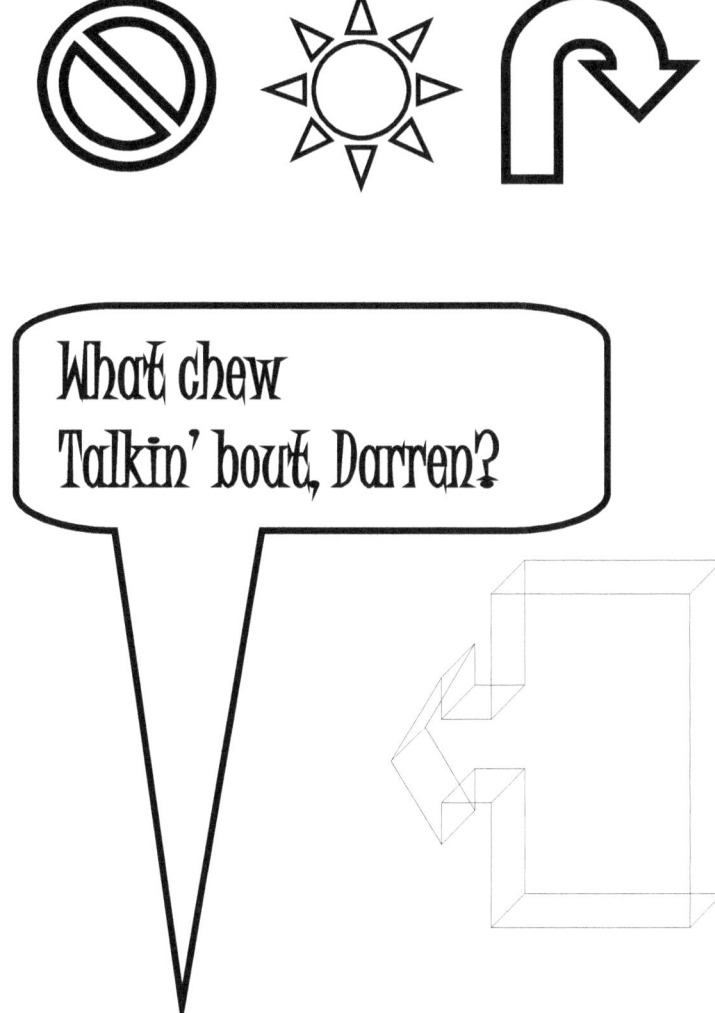

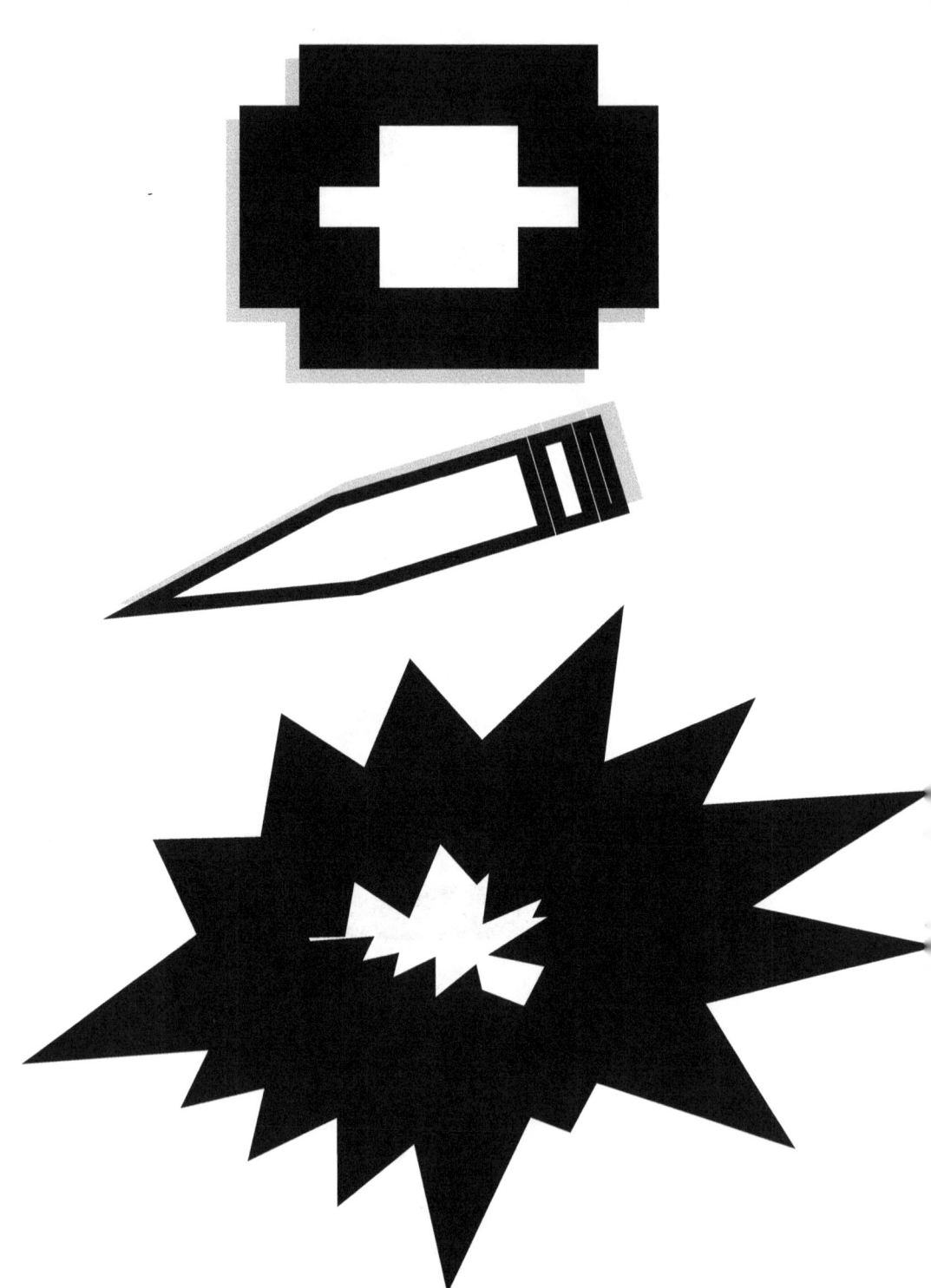

Why didn't you just say so?

About Darren Simon:

Darren Simon is currently studying linguistics at Vancouver Island University in Nanaimo, B.C. Poetry is merely a hobby for him, while the structure of language is his passion.

About Defeat:

I don't know about you, but it's depressing to me knowing that I would get beaten by a retard in the 300 meter hurdles at the Special Olympics.

About Satan:

I'm kinda surprised Satan hasn't gotten a bigger following over the years. The dude stands for everything worth living for ~ sex, drugs, money, power. Oh wait, he does have a pretty big following. But he's not worshipped. Oh wait, everything he stands for is worshipped. I'm confused.

Nemoi Enpoj

If you see a mirror,
will you look?
And if you look,
is it to admire your beauty?
Or do you marvel drop-jawed at your own hideousness.
Me:
I sometimes stare at myself and imagine I'm a washed-up celebrity.
Other times:
I fart, smile bashfully, and imagine I'm a tuba player in a half-time marching band.

My Dinner
Nemoi Enpoj

∞ InFiNitY ...
π   PiE ⊕
7 x 33 ±™÷Ω≠

```
Forget formula,
Abolish math,
Watery Soup. Soft daikon and stale scentless
onions. Add slimy mushrooms.
Recipe:
Like this, like this, like this.
Crumbling charcoal.
Dead penis.
Numb vagina.
Pickled liver.
This is my dinner
This is our lives.
```

About Nemoi Enpoj:

Nemoi resides in Budapest, Hungry with his two children and wife. He studied engineering at university and now works for a tin manufacturer. He writes poetry in his spare time.

Impressions of an Ex-Pat
Shannon Lyndsy

O Canada,

If only your utopian promises were true.

O Canada,

How many do you let die waiting in your emergency rooms?

O Canada,

You taught me with dog eared hand-me-down textbooks filled with lies that used to be true.

O Canada,

You'll be the first to put warning labels on junk food.

O Canada,

One day you will regulate everything we do.

O Canada,

Why do your people never challenge you?

O Canada,

How much more propaganda can you spew?

O Canada,

Now I understand why no one really bothered to claim you.

O Canada,

Your slimy hands are always in my pockets, while your badges are shoving their fists up my ass trying to pull a fine out of my bowels.
O Canada,
That red maple leaf should be replaced with the silhouette of a thief.
O Canada,
You made me too lazy, apathetic, and too inadequate to argue.
O Canada,
You've made 14 million laws to rule 33 million people.
O Canada,
From space you look like a bully-monster sitting on a throne at the top of the world.
O Canada,
You'll be the first to tax me for breathing and basking in the sun.
O Canada,
Oh, Oh, Canada.
How did you ever convince me I'm free?

Eternal Death
Shannon Lyndsy

If I'm truly, truly cursed, Christians are right,
life won't end with death,
I'll be stuck with this sick voice in my head that my parents gave a name to until the universe expands itself into extinction.
If I pray for anything, I pray that when I'm dead, I'm dead.
No more me. No more anybody. I don't want to live forever,
And I certainly don't want to be stuck in eternity with these people.
If there's a heaven, and they're all there, don't put me on the guest list, leave me standing in line.
Leave me in limbo, ignorant to the mysteries of life.
Leave me happily believing that there isn't any mystery.
Leave me with my nihilism.
Leave me with my neutralism.
Leave me in this Dionysian state of excess and depraved indifference,

slithering through the mushy black bowels of existence,

trying to find my way back into the hemorrhaging red cunt that I came screaming out of.

About Shannon Lyndsy

Shannon Lyndsy is the author of Generation Z, and has used a multitude of pseudonyms to express his THOUGHTS on barbecklit.com. More importantly, Shannon has 739 Facebook friends, over 12000 likes, and has been de-friended 7 times due to inappropriate wall-postings. He has recently gotten tested for HIV and is anxiously awaiting the results. In the meantime, he is searching Linked-In for qualified people to start a cult with.

the way of the world .
Shannon Shuster

in the absence of light
we disconnect
have time to recollect
things forgotten
things of the past

overcome by disbelief
repression giving way
wrath building
out of the horror
the horror

humanity
at a standstill
predacious
all the while
vulnerable

overcompensated belligerence
masking supposed weakness

the way of the world
in the absence of light
rape kill destroy

trigger.
Shannon Shuster

you push
and you press
never letting up
with a sharpie as my quill
i scratch the word trigger
from my collarbone
to the bottom of my ribcage
taking hold of your wrist
i run your hand
across my naked body
and place your finger
on my chest
hoping that one day
you'll change your tactics
and pull

About Shannon Shuster:

Shannon Shuster is an artist and writer out of Toronto, Canada. A riot grrrl at heart, she continually challenges societal norms and refuses to conform. Shannon loves art in all forms and appreciates humanity's desire to create.

TRAMP! TRAMP! TRAMP!
Howie Good

1

I was born on a cold day sixty years ago today. Something wrong? everyone who happens upon me asks. I remember the bottle of pills in my pocket. May cause drowsiness, the label says. Let's hope so. The pills are more pink than red. I pop one. It's how they do things here. Ten minutes pass. There are still many mentally ill New Yorkers. I pop another. The ground trembles with the footfalls of the rain tramping up from the South.

2

The same young nurse woke me every fifteen minutes to check my vitals, the flowers on the wallpaper opening just a crack. I looked away. The sun was coming up, naked and shivering. A burning freight train crawled endlessly through the background. There are probably better words to describe it, but I have been broken and mended and broken again.

3

Is it still winter there where you are? Do you have a dancing monkey to help you get through it? Here everything calls out to everything else. Nobody regrets that the first paint was probably animal blood. Only the birds seem kind of glum, black-capped chickadees with pebbles for eyes.

PORNOCUPIA
Howie Good

It's fashionable
to die young
and be pessimistic.

I myself prefer
a Vicodin
to the present,

until later,
when we're anointing
the bed,

your breasts
floating above me

like the pink
and green
sunsets

found only
in Ireland.

About Howie Good:

Howie Good, a journalism professor at SUNY New Paltz, is the author of the new poetry collection, Dreaming in Red, from Right Hand Pointing. He is also the author of numerous chapbooks, including most recently *The Devil's Fuzzy Slippers* from Flutter Press and Per*sonal Myths* from Writing Knights Press. He has another chapbook, *Fog Area*, forthcoming from Dog on a Chain Press.

About Vanity:

Doctors say that we shouldn't encourage the use of tanning beds 'cause they increase the odds of getting cancer. I say fuck that, let's double down and build more, they're like bug zappers for the vain and vapid.

About Why We Shouldn't Kiss Dogs:

Man sits on toilet. Dog drinks outta toilet. No more kissy-kiss.

A Time of Innocence
Tony Mulas

Compromising my good looks
by drinking
on an endless tab (with
an over-taxed liver and eggs
on the menu) I look back
to a more innocent time:

She was from Portugal
and was considered ugly
by one co-worker of mine, Dave the Slav
(who'd rather have food injected
into his system he said
to avoid having to eat),
but I liked her, her golden locks
which made for a sunny smile,
her Monroe figure, thin knees
though voluptuous and glabrous thighs
and hips in hot pants
her midriff exposed by a shirt

not buttoned but
simply done up in a bow--
a Western gal free in her skin
washing the Chrysler in the driveway.

She was also desirous
on the three occasions we were somewhat
alone (hidden amongst stacks of
concrete blocks in the excavation
of a new basement in her neighbourhood;
on the empty livingroom rug
while my parents were overseas
and while her friends frolicked outside--
I am not kissing and telling here
because nothing ever happened--
Confederation Park on the lawn
amongst the conspiring trees)
however very mindful, unlike me,
when the zippered moment was
about to become heated, that's
when she would break loose,
compose herself and run away. She
never told me on the phone (but

not her home phone) why she
wouldn't meet me ever again;
probably because she was Catholic
and I a future atheist.

I worked in her house
(raised the fireplace mantle with
a rowlock of brick and an everlasting
limestone ledge praised by W.H. Auden)
met her parents, and
got a cold bottle
of Labatt's 50 from her father
that summer. I reminisce
that he was the strict type,
cool amongst the guys but
he had killed me
and disowned his daughter
had I got her pregnant unwed.
That's why we met clandestinely
because he must have really
instilled some fear in her, a girl
about my age, and whose name I forget
but whose softness I remember.

It was the time I had
brought my first
cigarette home, to my old
dreary and dirty apartment, empty save
for a child's bed, drafting board
and juvenile desk. I remember
that strong smelly Export 'A'
got me well nigh stoned--
like marijuana I later learned.
I was practice smoking--and
coughing--now and then at work
all that week;
that only cigarette (given to me)
made for quite
a relaxant that evening,
the evening I last spoke
to my Portuguese love.

Mr. Baraxa
Tony Mulas

Mr. Baraxa lived alone in apartment 603,
whom I really don't know much about, and yet
somehow am moved to write his obituary
that'll be brief and stored, or lost, in the annals
                of the whodunnit.

Harried and days on end spent in a withering black
since it is no lie that Mr.Baraxa for the longest time
had the suspicious Hamilton police on his back,
interrogating him concerning the murder of his wife,
                an unsolved crime.

He, though, proved irascible as investigators could not
pin on him, what in dark corridors of his building
fellow tenants whispered: "oh he did not get caught,
for possibly hiring thugs, that in the cover of night...
                did the killing!"

Perhaps, perhaps, an Othellian tale of rage and jealousy,
for it is widely stated that Baraxa's wife was beautiful,
and a cashier at a gas station where the daft conspiracy
transpired, in Hamilton, again, during the wee hours when
                thieves are plentiful.

Either out of compunction or a sincere loneliness
that these many onward years did an alcoholic Baraxa
play the curmudgeon, always sarcastically swearing at us
as we worked around the building and as he always left
                in a taxi.

How he was found dead deserves some lines of noteworthy,
for the stench of Death, like an invisible pervasive smoke,
was seeping out from his apartment door number 603
down the hall and dark passageways of rumour, for it
                was no joke.

It was, however, a skinny Roberta doing her janitorial rounds
who decided to knock on Death's quiescent wood door
and knock knock again, knock knock to no peep or sound,
for Monsieur La Mort answers to nobody, as much as
                Roberta did implore.

Thus motivated by no response and a horrible putrefaction,
Roberta, the skinny and distraught superintendent, flees
the sixth-floor hall abandoning her vacuum in dejection,
down the elevator to her apartment to retrieve another set
                of Baraxa's keys.

Having returned hastily, Roberta was eerily right
to have the worst on her mind, so bravely enter
apartment 603 she did that Friday morn, bright
as it was outdoors, yet still a hard-working day for
                Death, no matter.

So could you imagine the slaughterhouse stench
when a retching Roberta opened the door? Death this time
grotesquely ballooning and blackening his victim; every inch
of intestine spilt, a cadaver split open by gaseous Death
                compounding the crime.

The authorities soon sequestered apartment 603,
the coroner ruling Mr. Baraxa suffered a heart attack
while sitting on the toilet, his age being around 73,
a handsome Hungarian immigrant, bereft unto a life
                shackled to black.

Yes indeed, Death painted a gruesome-enough masterpiece,
forcing his deceased and swelling male model to sit askew,
darken horribly and burst in a finale of life's short lease;
Death working in the air-conditioning, avoiding maggots midst
                the bloody stew.

The authorities, or call them Death's meticulous curators,
told a smoking and tipsy Roberta that poor Mr. Baraxa
sat stiff for five days, thus postponing Heaven's negotiators
who in prayer and sermon say you cannot escape
                death and taxes.

As neatly as the funereal innards were cleaned up,
Baraxa's blood had seeped under the old vinyl floor
tiles that Ronnie, Big Jim and myself had to take up
and renovate in a thick malodorous air that invaded
                your every core.

Coincidently, Mr. Baraxa's brother just died a week
previous, and so it remained that there appeared
no one, not even from Hungary, mournful and meek,
to claim the belongings of a man who walked with a cane
                yet was feared.

When I was trashing his personal effects at the city
dump: cloths and photo albums and cheap bric-a-brac,
I kind of thought it wasn't night or right, and felt a pity
for Mr. Baraxa, cantankerous general, sullied forever
                in shadows black.

About Tony Mulas:

Tony Mulas runs his own construction company and often plays hooky from work to pursue a dream that just doesn't seem to be real to him: Poetry. Most of his poems are autobiographical and based on true life experiences. He lives in Hamilton, Canada with his young son and loving wife, Anna.

One Last Thought, About Beauty:

There must be beauty contained in the repulsive and revolting things in this world. Otherwise, they wouldn't captivate us. We wouldn't stare at car accidents, or gaze awestruck at an unattractive person, or look online at pictures of STD's, or leer with fascination at morbidly obese people at the beach. Indeed, sometimes ugliness is more entrancing than conventional beauty.

Also available from
BareBackPress

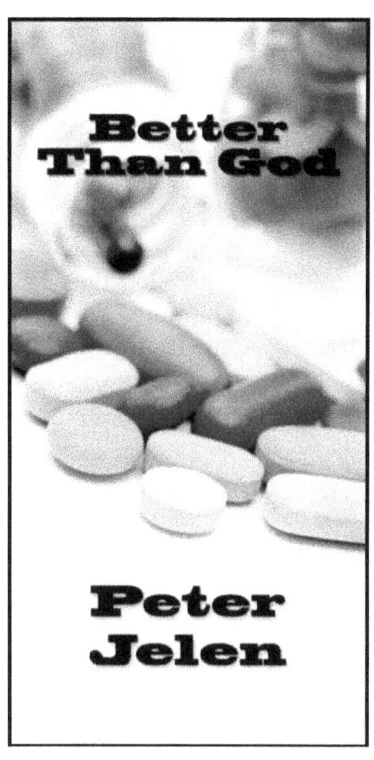

Better Than God
Peter Jelen

ONLY HUMANS CAN BE
HUMANE

Michael's father is steadily deteriorating from Alzheimer's. In his rare moments of lucidity, he begs for death. As much as Michael wants to believe that his father's pleas are part of the disease, he knows in his heart, that they are a suffering man's last wish. How can Michael help his father die…peacefully?

Better Than God is a collection of dark and humorous fast paced, imaginative stories, like *Menting*, *Survival of the Swiftest*, and *Confining the Critic*.

$18.99
ISBN 13: 978-0988075016
254 Pages
BIASC: Short Stories

www.barebackpress.com

Generation Z
Shannon Lyndsy

ENVIRONMENTALISM IS SPREADING ACROSS THE WORLD LIKE FACEBOOK. MORE AND MORE PEOPLE ARE GOING GREEN, AND NOT JUST FOR THE SEX.

It's the beginning of the end of the world and Sean Logan thinks he has the power to stop it. As a member of Generation Z, a group of HIV positive environmentalists who have willfully contracted the disease in order to depopulate the planet and save Earth from further human harm, Sean crusades to convert as many people as possible, spreading the cure, and preaching the message of Generation Z ~ for the greater good.

$18.99
ISBN 13: 978-0988075030
244 Pages
BISAC: Fiction

www.barebackpress.com

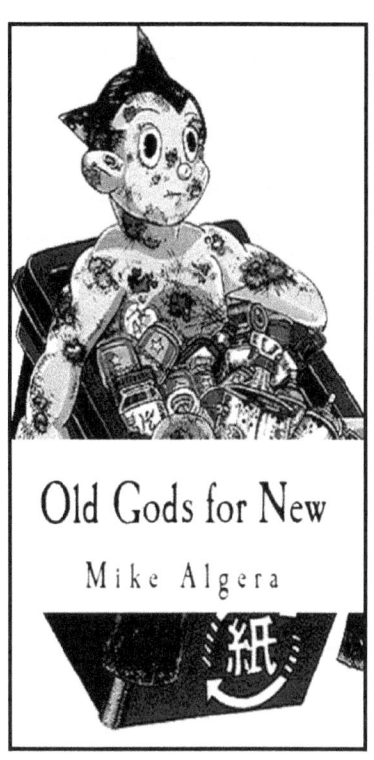

**Old Gods for New
Mike Algera**

At a sidewalk sale
you will meet a dealer
he will tell you
he has monuments of old gods
for sale, "Pick a God,
and worship however you please."

Old Gods for New reflects upon personal triumphs and demons, love and longing, the past and never-was; musings that spark both the artistry of playful banter as well as lyrical madness. Writing that is quirky yet daring, combining scratch words into something new.

$19.99
ISBN 13: 978-0988075075
138 Pages
BISAC: Poetry

www.barebackpress.com

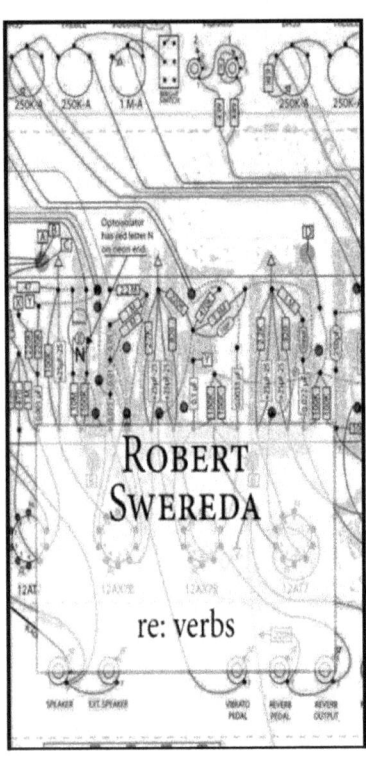

Robert Swereda
re: verbs

-regarding verbs
-reverberating texts and their actions
-"re" as in redo, rerun, reread, reconsider

The texts of re: verbs raises questions of the flexibility of language, its boundaries, limitations, frustrations. The use of found text, the poetics of erasure, linguistic investigation, flarf and visual poetry.

$18.00
ISBN 13: 978-0988075054
132 Pages
BISAC: Poetry

www.barebackpress.com

www.ingramcontent.com/pod-product-compliance
Lightning Source LLC
Chambersburg PA
CBHW060153100426
42744CB00007B/1006